Contents

Bikes and trikes

It's fun to ride a bike or a trike!

Ding

Ding

Toys I play with

Outside toys

Barbara Hunter

Heinemann
LIBRARY

Little Nippers

www.heinemann.co.uk/library
Visit our website to find out more information about **Heinemann Library** books.

To order:
☎ Phone 44 (0) 1865 888066
▤ Send a fax to 44 (0) 1865 314091
💻 Visit the Heinemann Bookshop at www.heinemann.co.uk/library to browse our catalogue and order online.

First published in Great Britain by Heinemann Library, Halley Court, Jordan Hill, Oxford OX2 8EJ, part of Harcourt Education.
Heinemann is a registered trademark of Harcourt Education Ltd.

Editorial: Jilly Attwood and Claire Throp
Design: Jo Hinton-Malivoire and bigtop, Bicester, UK
Models made by: Jo Brooker
Picture Research: Catherine Bevan
Production: Lorraine Warner

Originated by Dot Gradations
Printed and bound in China by South China Printing Company

ISBN 0 431 16341 3 (hardback)
06 05 04 03 02
10 9 8 7 6 5 4 3 2 1

ISBN 0 431 16346 4 (paperback)
06 05 04 03 02
10 9 8 7 6 5 4 3 2 1

British Library Cataloguing in Publication Data
Hunter, Barbara
Outside toys. – (Toys I play with)
790.1'33
A full catalogue record for this book is available from the British Library.

Acknowledgements
The publishers would like to thank the following for permission to reproduce photographs:
Angela Hampton p. **5**; Bubbles p. **4** (Ian Lever), p. **21** (Ian West); Lupe Cuhna p. **8-9**; Sally and Richard Greenhill pp. **10-11**, **14**, **20**; Tudor Photography pp. **6-7**, **12**, **13**, **15**, **16**, **17**, **18**, **19**.

Cover photograph reproduced with permission of Gareth Boden.

The publishers would like to thank Annie Davy for her assistance in the preparation of this book.

Every effort has been made to contact copyright holders of any material reproduced in this book. Any omissions will be rectified in subsequent printings if notice is given to the publishers.

If you pedal hard you can go really **FAST**.

5

Scooter

You need to push really hard with one foot when you ride a scooter.

Swing

WWheeee!

Climbing frame

Can you climb to the top of a metal climbing frame?

You can hang,
swing and
climb through
the spaces.

11

Skipping rope and hula hoop

If you learn to turn the rope quickly you can skip very fast.

Can you get a plastic hula hoop to turn
round and round your waist?

Bats and balls

How far can
you hit a ball
with a bat?

Whack!

Paddling pool and sand pit

Do you like splashing in water in the hot weather?

Can you make a sandcastle
in the sand pit?

Playhouse

Sometimes you can pretend to be inside when you are outside!

Gardening

It's fun to
dig in the
garden.

digging

planting

You can plant
seeds and bulbs.

Actions

splashing

digging

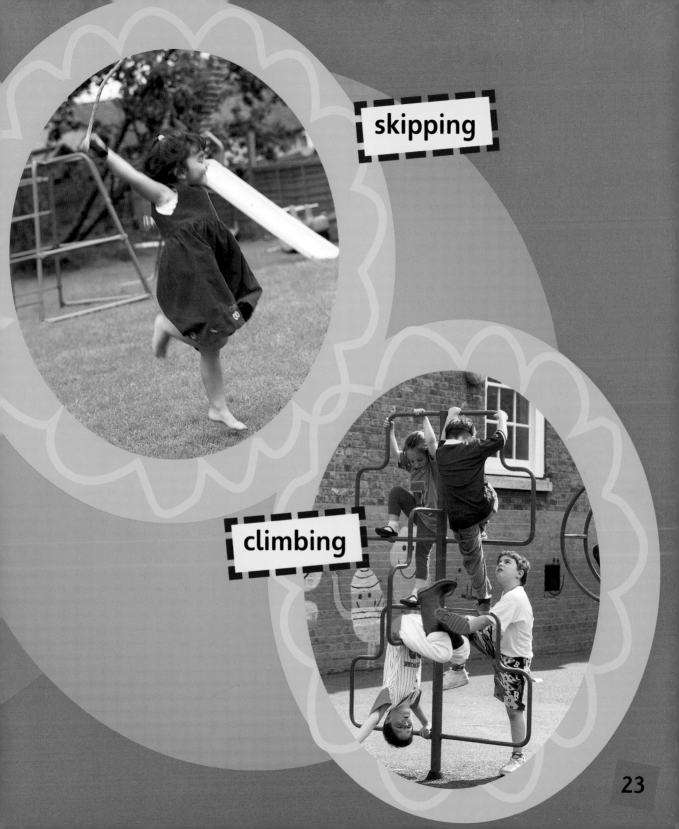

skipping

climbing

23

Index

The end

Notes for adults

This series supports the young child's knowledge and understanding of their world. The following Early Learning Goals are relevant to the series:
• find out about, and identify, some features of living things, objects and events that they observe;
• exploration and investigation: feeling textures and materials.

The series explores a range of different play experiences by looking at features of different toys and the materials they are made from. **Outside Toys** includes things made from the following materials: metal, plastic, rubber, rope and fabric. Some of the experiences featured in this book include being in a large space, playing with other children, physical activity including pushing and pulling, and skills that take practice to achieve. Mathematical language like fast/slow, high/low, under/through can also be explored.

There is an opportunity for the child to compare and contrast the different kinds of play as well as relating them to their own experiences. They may be encouraged to realize they have mastered some skills like riding a bike although they may still need more practice in others, like bouncing a ball or skipping.

Follow-up activities

By making direct reference to the book the child can be encouraged to try new experiences, e.g. throwing and catching a ball, or splashing in the paddling pool like the children in the book. Taking photographs of the activities would be an excellent way for the child to start making their own book.